LANCASHI… …RLAND'S LAST DAYS… …Y STEAM

b… …Heavyside

As far as steam locomotives were concerned, during the 1970s and early 1980s the National Coal Board North Western Area mainly relied on a batch of Hunslet 'Austerity' 0-6-0STs. Their *raison d'être* had been the urgent need for a robust, powerful, yet easily maintained shunting locomotive to assist the Allied forces overseas, as well as on the home front, during the Second World War. The doyen of the class was released from the Hunslet Engine Company's Jack Lane Works in Leeds on 1 January 1943, and they proved so successful that construction continued long after the war had ceased, no less than 485 being built, with the last one not until 1964. On 1 January 1970 the NCB had twenty dispersed about Lancashire and Cumberland, fourteen manufactured by Hunslet themselves, along with two each from the factories of Hudswell Clarke of Leeds, Robert Stephenson & Hawthorns of Newcastle-upon-Tyne, and the Vulcan Foundry at Newton-le-Willows, Lancashire. They comprised four which had been handed down to the NCB by their previous owners at Vesting Day, 1 January 1947, thirteen purchased new from Hunslet between 1950 and 1957, and three bought second-hand, one in 1947 and two in 1965. This is 'Hurricane', Hunslet works No. 3830, built in 1955, pictured at Bickershaw Colliery, Leigh, on 13 June 1974.

Acknowledgements

My sincere thanks are due to Paul Abell, Gordon Blears, Geoff Creese, Bob Darvill, John Fozard, Richard Greenwood, Roger Hateley, Geoffrey Hayes, Peter Holmes, Ivor Thomas and the staff of Wigan Heritage Service for their ready assistance during the completion of this volume.

First published in the United Kingdom, 2007,
by Stenlake Publishing Ltd.
www.stenlake.co.uk
ISBN 9781840333916

The power of an 'Austerity' 0-6-0ST is ably demonstrated by Hunslet works No. 3694 of 1950, 'Whiston', as it hauls a couple of 'merry-go-round' wagons up a 1-in-17 gradient at Bold Colliery, St Helens, on 20 August 1974.

INTRODUCTION

While a very limited amount of the coal beneath the surface of south and east Lancashire and west Cumberland had been used as a fuel for centuries, its bulk and weight usually precluded its use other than in the immediate locality to where it was excavated. In time those pits situated relatively close to a navigable waterway or port, such as those served by the Leeds & Liverpool and Bridgewater canals in Lancashire, or near to the harbour at Whitehaven, came to have a distinct advantage, since the raw material could be conveniently loaded into barges or sea-going vessels. However, it was the laying of the main line railway network and the development of the steam locomotive from the middle years of the nineteenth century that proved the real catalyst for the rapid expansion of the coal industry. Now, the black gold could be moved economically and efficiently over land, as well as by water, to wherever it was needed for either industrial or domestic consumption.

Following the nationalisation of the coal industry in Britain on 1 January 1947, the state-owned National Coal Board, like its predecessors, continued to rely mainly on steam locomotives for its motive power needs. However, in common with British Railways, by the 1960s steam's dominance was declining, many engines being made redundant due to pit closures, the introduction of road haulage or conveyor belt systems, while others were superseded by diesel locomotives.

By the late 1960s, a period during which British Railways eliminated steam locomotives from its normal services (Lancashire being the last stronghold), it was becoming increasingly obvious that steam had a very limited future on the lines owned by the NCB. Such was the decimation of the iron horse that by 1 January 1970 only thirty-four steam locomotives were listed amongst the assets of the NCB in the two counties, eighteen in Lancashire and sixteen in Cumberland. While in Lancashire fifteen diesel locomotives handled a large proportion of the work at this time, in contrast steam still had sole charge of the railway operations in Cumberland, although in that county only two deep-mine collieries remained in production.

In Lancashire at the start of the 1970s the steam shunting and trip workings were almost exclusively handled by a fleet of fourteen 'Austerity' 0-6-0STs designed by the Hunslet Engine Company of Leeds, a class first introduced in 1943 under the direction of the Ministry of Supply, although some of those at work in the county had been built as late as 1955. The other four engines, all with an 0-4-0 wheel arrangement, similarly carried their water supplies in a saddle tank, the eldest, 'King', at Bank Hall Colliery, Burnley, having been put together by Andrew Barclay Sons & Co. Ltd of Kilmarnock in 1919. The remaining three 0-4-0s, all dating from the mid-1930s, two built by Hawthorn Leslie of Newcastle-upon-Tyne and one by Peckett's of Bristol, were regrettably simply awaiting an appointment with a scrap merchant.

There was a slightly different picture in west Cumberland where the stock had a much more cosmopolitan flavour, the locomotives having originated from the factories of eight independent locomotive builders between 1905 and 1957. Listed on the registers were eight 0-4-0STs and seven 0-6-0STs, the latter including six 'Austerities', while based at Harrington Coal Preparation Plant at Lowca, near Whitehaven, was the only 0-6-0 side tank in the area, 'Unity', constructed by Hudswell Clarke & Co. Ltd of Leeds in 1927.

A distinctive feature atop many locomotives in the north west at this time was an oblong chimney which tapered inwards, indicating the engine was fitted with a Giesl ejector, the brainchild of Austrian locomotive engineer Dr Adolph Giesl-Gieslingen. Basically, the modification provided a more efficient exhaust blast, with a consequent improvement in performance, a saving in fuel costs, and a cleaner exhaust. Eighteen NCB locomotives in Lancashire were so equipped in the 1960s and from 1967 a number migrated north to Cumberland.

By January 1976 only eight steam locomotives remained on the books of the NCB in Cumberland, although in reality the engines were all simply lying idle, with railway operations in the county having ceased the previous year, Haig Colliery at Whitehaven being the last outpost. Steam's position in the Red Rose county, where eleven 'Austerities' could be found, was much more encouraging, with Bickershaw Colliery, Leigh, and Bold Colliery, St Helens, both totally dependent on steam. In fact, in order to bolster the stock at these two collieries, four 'Austerities' were transferred into Lancashire between 1974 and 1978, two from North Wales and two from Staffordshire.

In the event, both Bickershaw and Bold continued to rely on steam until well into the 1980s, even though at the former colliery it was relegated to a standby role from the winter of 1979 when a couple of diesels arrived. In practice, one of the Bickershaw 'Austerities' was usually active at least once a week while the diesels were serviced or otherwise unavailable, the last steam turn being worked by Hunslet works No. 3776 of 1952 in October 1983. At Bold the 'Austerities' retained command until a diesel took over in September 1982, although Hunslet works No. 3163 of 1944, 'Joseph', was subsequently brought out of retirement for a few days at the end of September/beginning of October 1983.

Today, coal mining in the two counties in the traditional manner - whereby men descended hundreds of feet into the bowels of the earth to crawl along narrow passageways in order to win coal - is a thing of the past. However, as a reminder of the methods of days gone by, some of the surface buildings, including one of the headstocks at both Astley Green Colliery, Tyldesley, near Manchester, and Haig Colliery, Whitehaven, have been retained at what are now museum complexes dedicated to the mining industry. Furthermore, nine of the locomotives that saw service in the north west during the 1970s and early 1980s managed to escape the clutches of the scrap metal merchants and have been saved for future generations to enjoy, albeit in much more sanitised surroundings than in the past.

On a personal note, visiting the steam locations on the west Cumberland coast usually meant an overnight stay, while the Lancashire pits were conveniently situated just a few miles from home. This was especially so in the case of Bickershaw Colliery at Leigh where I regularly dashed after work in order to imbibe steam for a couple of hours or so. There I became friendly with one of the drivers, the late Harold Gillibrand, and when the weather was not too kind for photography I would accompany him on the footplate, every now and then being told to grab the shovel and throw a round or two of coal into the firebox, while on one notable occasion I was privileged to handle the regulator on the climb up to the BR exchange sidings. Was there any better way to spend an evening? Bold, too, holds special memories, insomuch that due to the kindness of a friend who was an official there, I was able to enjoy a conducted tour beneath the surface. There I witnessed the harsh realities the workforce faced each day, as had hundreds of thousands of miners down the years. In many ways society owes an incalculable debt to these men. I hope that the ensuing pages will provide a suitable tribute to those days and convey at least something of the rugged nature of the collieries during the latter days of steam.

NCB driver Harold Gillibrand looks out from the cab of an 'Austerity' at Bickershaw Colliery, Leigh, on 18 August 1972. The lettering surrounding the crest - 'National Coal Board N.W. Division' - refers to the NCB administrative structure prior to 26 March 1967. From that date the collieries in Lancashire and Cumberland all became part of a newly created North Western Area, before this was absorbed into the Western Area on 1 April 1974.

A moment of glory. Each day of the Spring Bank Holiday weekend, 24 to 26 May 1980, British Rail celebrated the 150th anniversary of the Liverpool & Manchester Railway with a grand procession of locomotives and stock along the section of line used for the historic Rainhill trials in October 1829. Bold Colliery sidings, conveniently situated a little way to the east, were used as a base for the event. Lined up alongside a number of prestigious locomotives such as 'Flying Scotsman', 'Duchess of Hamilton' and 'Evening Star', and replicas of the entrants for the 1829 trials, 'Rocket', 'Sans Pareil' and 'Novelty', was Bold 'Austerity' Hudswell Clarke works No. 1752, 'Robert', built in 1943. Here, suitably smartened up for the occasion, a proud 'Robert' has just been flagged past the official cavalcade starting point, ready to be greeted by thousands of spectators in the specially erected stands. Following at a safe distance is Ivatt Class 4MT 2-6-0 No. 43106, normally to be seen on the Severn Valley Railway at Bridgnorth.

Nine of the NCB locomotives that worked in Lancashire and Cumberland in the 1970s have been saved for posterity, among them former Walkden and Whitehaven-based Giesl ejector-fitted Hunslet 'Austerity' 0-6-0ST works No. 3698, 'Repulse', built in 1950. This was transported to the Lakeside & Haverthwaite Railway in south Cumbria (formerly part of Lancashire) in September 1976 and to date the engine has recorded a grand total of 38,409 miles, hauling passenger trains along this privately owned three-and-a-half-mile ex-Furness Railway branch which had been closed by BR in September 1965. Looking immaculate in a somewhat different environment to that of its earlier life, 'Repulse' is seen here leaving the intermediate station at Newby Bridge while returning from Lakeside, near the southern tip of Lake Windermere, back to Haverthwaite on 16 October 1988.

The comparatively small but important coalfield in west Cumberland was concentrated around the coastal towns of Maryport, Workington and Whitehaven. In 1950 twelve collieries produced a combined total of 1,130,000 tons of coal and found employment for over 5,500 men. Ten years later, in 1960, the number of pits had been reduced to seven with some 4,000 men on the payroll, although productivity was slightly higher with over 950,000 tons being brought to the surface that year. However, by 1970 only two collieries remained - Haig at Whitehaven and the smaller Solway at Workington. Harrington No. 10 Colliery at Lowca, two miles north of Whitehaven, ceased winding in July 1968, but the coal preparation plant was retained to wash the output from Solway Colliery. The coal reached Harrington by way of the British Railways coast line as far as Parton, where it reversed in order to gain what were the last remnants of the ex-Whitehaven, Cleator & Egremont Railway's Parton to Distington branch. At the exchange sidings, where a second reversal was necessary, NCB locomotives took charge for the last half mile of the journey. Here, looking east towards the Lake District, Giesl ejector-fitted Hunslet 'Austerity' 0-6-0ST works No. 3778, 'Warspite', built in 1952, is seen climbing away from the exchange sidings with six 21-ton hopper wagons laden with Solway coal on 14 May 1971. In places the gradient was reputedly as steep as 1-in-25. The line in the right foreground formerly led to the closed Harrington No. 11 Colliery.

Photographed on the same day, 'Warspite' crosses the unclassified road that leads through Lowca and approaches the plant with more coal from Solway. Note the board by the entrance still proclaims this to be Harrington No. 10 Colliery, despite the fact that no coal had been wound there for nearly three years. Before being transferred to Harrington in November 1968, 'Warspite' was based at Walkden, near Manchester, and was one of six 'Austerities' selected from September 1959, along with a couple of ex-North Staffordshire Railway 0-6-2Ts, to burn a mixture of coke and coal in an endeavour to reduce black smoke emissions (see page 28). To accommodate the coke it was necessary to fit an extension to the bunkers on the 'Austerities', together with a dividing plate in order to keep the coal and coke separate. However, the experiment was soon abandoned and normal firing methods reinstated, although 'Warspite', as clearly identifiable in this illustration, retained its longer bunker so as to house a Hill-Bigwood mechanical stoker that was fitted in 1961. The Ship Inn, seen beyond the level crossing and frequented no doubt by many a thirsty Harrington miner over the years, has since been converted to a private dwelling.

'Warspite' bides time in front of the washery at Harrington, again on 14 May 1971. After processing, the majority of the coal was loaded from the bunker on the right and taken via the Lowca Light Railway back to Workington, to the then British Steel Corporation Moss Bay Iron & Steel Works. Harrington No. 10 Colliery was in fact sunk by a former owner of the Moss Bay Works, the Workington Iron & Steel Company. Work started in 1910, and to take advantage of the good quality coking coal on offer, a battery of Koppers Regenerative ovens were built alongside. Later, the steelworks, the associated collieries and their ancillary plants, along with the Lowca Light Railway, were taken over by the United Steel Company. When the colliery was vested in the NCB in January 1947 the USC retained ownership of the Lowca Light Railway and the coking plant, W.D. Becker ovens having superseded the original Koppers. At that time the plant was able to process up to 520,000 tons of coal per annum and, as well as coke, among the by-products produced were tar, sulphate of ammonia, rectified benzole and gas for industrial and town use.

The NCB crest that was applied to locomotives working in the North Western Area.

On 14 May 1971, with the day's work completed, 'Warspite' is about to be bedded down for the night in the large two-road engine shed at Harrington. Hidden from view inside the shed were a couple of 'Austerities' built by Vulcan Foundry of Newton-le-Willows, Lancashire, in 1945, works No. 5282, still sporting its old WD No. 187, and works No. 5297, 'Amazon'. Also in the shed was Hudswell Clarke 0-6-0T works No. 1587, 'Unity', of 1927, brought from Ifton Colliery, Weston Rhyn, near Oswestry, in May 1969. Both No. 187 and 'Unity' were scrapped during the autumn of 1971. The closure of Solway Colliery in May 1973 also spelt the end for the operation at Harrington and shortly afterwards both 'Amazon' and 'Warspite' were transported the short distance to Ladysmith shed at Whitehaven. Today, while much of the Harrington site remains derelict, a portion on the south side has been taken over by the Lowca Amateur Rugby League Football Club and includes a fine clubhouse.

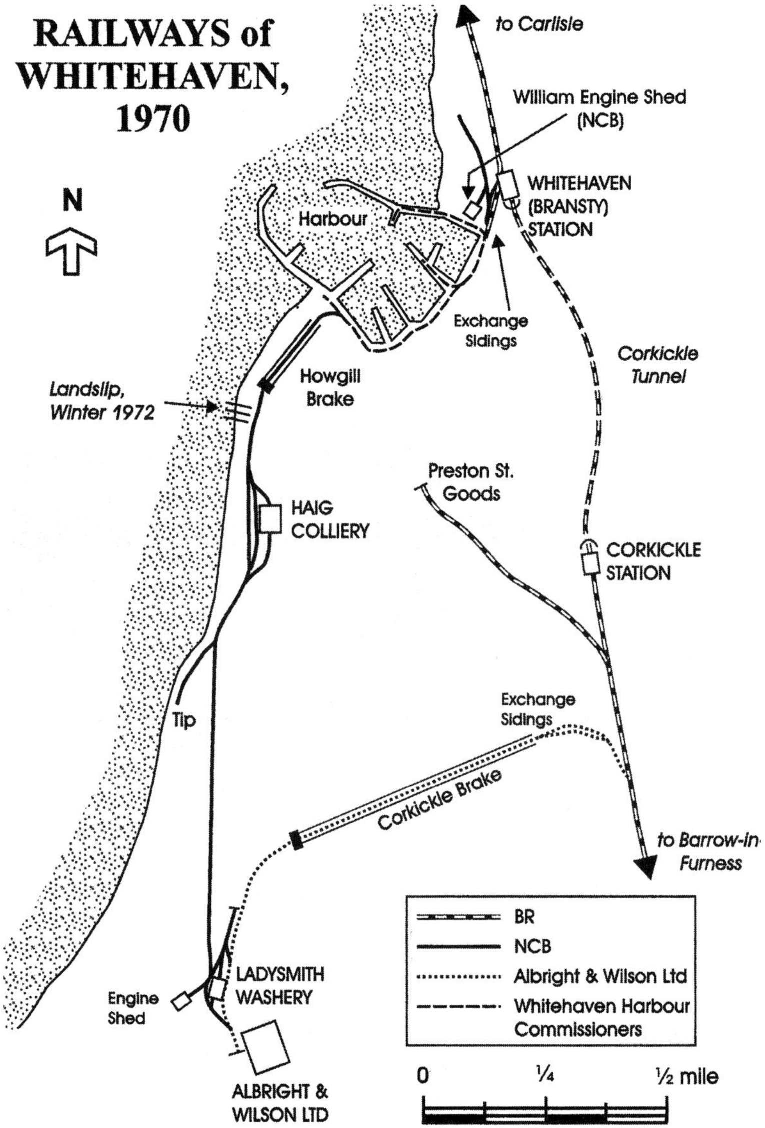

The beginnings of the railway infrastructure in Whitehaven can be traced back to 1735 when a short horse-and-gravity-operated wooden wagonway was opened on the south side of the town in order to carry coal to the harbour. The wagons were lowered to the harbour via a rope-worked incline known as the Howgill Brake. In 1774 the line was extended further south so as to serve the Croft Pit (near the future site of Ladysmith Colliery). The main line through the town was completed in September 1852 when the Whitehaven & Furness Junction Railway's route from the south was linked with the Whitehaven Junction Railway at Bransty, although it was December 1855 before it was opened for passenger trains, whereupon the W&FJR terminus at Preston Street (formerly Newtown) became goods only. A second exit from Croft, constructed in 1881 to what was then the Furness Railway, necessitated a further rope-worked incline - the Corkickle Brake. Croft Pit closed in 1903 after Ladysmith became operative.

In 1914 the Whitehaven Colliery Company, owners of Ladysmith, Wellington and William collieries (the latter two near the harbour) began the development of Haig Colliery, along with a new coking plant at Ladysmith to replace that at William. After the First World War the company suffered some very difficult years, resulting in the closure of Ladysmith in 1931, followed by Wellington and William the next year, before going into liquidation in 1933. Following a number of failed attempts to revive the collieries, the Cumberland Coal Company (Whitehaven) Ltd reopened Haig and William in 1937, only for the latter to close again in 1955. Meanwhile, in 1943, the expanding Marchon Products chemical company had taken possession of the former coking plant site at Ladysmith. They subsequently rebuilt the Corkickle Brake in 1955, the same year the business was taken over by Albright & Wilson Ltd.

The method of operation in NCB days was for the coal wound at Haig to be propelled to Ladysmith for washing before being dragged back to the top of the Howgill Brake. After reaching the Whitehaven Harbour Commissioners tracks the wagons were manoeuvred to one of the quays or the BR exchange sidings by Bransty Station. However, sometime during the miners strike of January/February 1972 the Howgill Brake was effectively rendered useless when a landslip, just to the north of Haig, severed the route to the incline. Overnight the NCB had to make new arrangements, with road haulage being introduced between Ladysmith and the harbour, while some spare capacity was utilised on the Corkickle Brake. The railway between Haig and Ladysmith remained operative until March 1975, when a fleet of lorries began shuttling between the two sites. In 1977 the preparation plant at Ladysmith was replaced by a new facility at Haig, with the coal subsequently being despatched to the harbour by a conveyor belt. The Corkickle Brake continued to serve the chemical works until November 1986.

Not far from the cliff edge at Whitehaven, at the north end of Haig Colliery, Giesl ejector-fitted Hunslet 'Austerity' works No. 3698, 'Repulse', built in 1950, draws a lengthy rake of loaded NCB internal hopper wagons away from the screens on 28 August 1973. In 1950 Haig paid the wages of 1,385 men (1,065 working underground and 320 on the surface) with 296,000 tons of coal being wrought from under the Irish Sea. Similar figures were recorded during the early 1970s. This particular 'Austerity' had been at Whitehaven for three months, having arrived on 28 May 1973 from the Walkden Railways, near Manchester, where it had been based since new.

Left: A few minutes after the picture on the previous page had been exposed and having reversed by the buffer stops, 'Repulse' starts out on the demanding one-mile climb to Ladysmith Washery. The site of the landslip which cut off the line to the Howgill Brake during the winter of 1972 is just behind the buffer stops. A wooden wagon stands isolated on the far side of the chasm, while just beyond is the Irish Sea and the entrance to Whitehaven Harbour. This was also the location where the 'Austerity' 'Respite' nearly met a premature end in November 1974 after running away from Ladysmith with some empty wagons, only coming to a halt in the nick of time near the edge of the precipice after demolishing the stop blocks. A few days later the engine was transported by road to Walkden Central Workshops, near Manchester, with a handwritten label attached marked 'for repair and return'. It never did return (see page 33).

Opposite: Andrew Barclay 0-4-0ST works No. 1448, 'King', pauses between duties at Haig Colliery on 30 August 1974. The locomotive, destined to spend most of its life in Lancashire, was delivered from the manufacturer's Caledonia Works in Kilmarnock to Ashton's Green Colliery, St Helens, in October 1919. After this colliery closed in 1930, 'King' next worked in 1934, first for a brief period at Welch Whittle Colliery, Coppull (north of Wigan), followed by a more permanent move to Ashton Moss Colliery, Audenshaw (east of Manchester), later that same year. From November 1959 it was at Bank Hall Colliery, Burnley, where it acquired a Giesl ejector, before a final transfer (via Walkden Central Workshops) to Whitehaven in May 1972. The engine was equipped with 14in. diameter outside cylinders with a 22in. stroke and 3ft 5in. diameter wheels. Note, too, the engine has two sets of sandboxes, enabling sand to be spread in front of the wheels whether running in forward or reverse gear. The cast nameplates attached to the saddle tank in its earlier days had by this time been replaced by painted wooden versions as seen here. The Andrew Barclay works plates had also been removed from the cab sides.

KING
4739/1667

With the colliery buildings at Haig in the background and paying scant regard to the provisions of the 1956 Clean Air Act, 'Repulse' powers yet more coal towards the washery at Ladysmith on 30 August 1974. 'Repulse' was a member of the Hunslet-designed 'Austerity' class which had 18in. x 26in. inside cylinders and 4ft 3in. diameter wheels set to a rigid wheelbase of 11ft 0in., enabling them to negotiate curves with a radius of 180ft with ease. The boilers could maintain pressure up to 170lb. per square inch, providing a nominal tractive effort of 23,870lb. at 85% of maximum boiler pressure, although the Hunslet catalogue quoted 21,060lb. at 75% pressure. The saddle tanks held up to 1,200 gallons of water and the bunkers two and a quarter tons of coal, the total weight in full working order being 48 tons 4cwt. It was recommended that they run on rails of not less than 80lb. per yard. The engines were designed to haul a load of 1,120 tons along level track, 565 tons up a gradient of 1-in-100 and 320 tons up an incline as steep as 1-in-50. They were ideal workhorses for the harsh working environment at Whitehaven.

Hunslet 'Austerity' works No. 3696, 'Respite', built in 1950, makes its way south light engine from Haig back to Ladysmith on 28 August 1973. The hopper wagons on the left are laden with colliery waste ready for depositing on the beach. Haig had the distinction of being the last deep-mine colliery in Cumberland but, pleasingly, after it closed in 1986 the set of headgear nearest the camera and the winding house were retained. They now form part of a museum the aim of which is to commemorate the past and remind future generations of an industry that was once paramount to the economic well-being of the area. Appropriately, the 0-4-0ST 'Askham Hall' has been housed here in recent years, the locomotive originally having been supplied new to the Whitehaven Colliery Co. Ltd by the Bristol-based Avonside Engine Co. Ltd in 1917 as their works No. 1772. In the past it had spells working at both Ladysmith and William collieries, as well as at Solway Colliery, Workington, and St Helens Colliery, Siddick, near Workington. It last worked from William shed in 1972.

Opposite: Midway up the bank between Haig and Ladysmith, a convoy of hopper wagons, with 'Repulse' pounding away at the rear, slowly make their way past a cluster of miners' cottages on 28 August 1973. In the background, across the Irish Sea, can be discerned the Scottish coastline, while by looking out to the west the Isle of Man, the destination for much Whitehaven coal over the years, could be seen. The former trackbed now forms part of the long-distance Cumbria Coastal Path, although the Haig Colliery Mining Museum have designs on relaying the rails along this section with a view to operating steam locomotives in the future as an added museum attraction.

Right: The concrete washer at Ladysmith, viewed from the footplate of Hunslet 'Austerity' works No. 3302, 'Stanley', on 13 May 1971. The engine was supplied by Hunslet to Manchester Collieries in August 1945 and, except for a few months from November 1961, when it was at Chanters Colliery, Tyldesley, it remained on the Walkden Railways until it was transferred to Whitehaven at the beginning of 1971.

Opposite: With steam seemingly leaking from every gland, 'King' hardly appears in the best of health as it musters all its strength at Ladysmith on 30 August 1974. It was stopped with a cracked firebox at the end of the year and scrapped during the autumn of 1976.

Right: Flanked by some NCB nine-plank wooden wagons, 'Stanley' prepares to move a rake of BR 21-ton hoppers of washed coal down the gradient to the top of the Howgill Brake on 13 May 1971. The leading wagon is clearly marked 'house coal concentration', while the second wagon has had overhead electrification warning plates attached.

With the washer on the left, 'Respite' shunts at Ladysmith on 28 August 1973. The overhead gantry conveyed waste from the plant for tipping off the coast. The one-road engine shed is the building next to the end on the right-hand side of the picture. The approach was by a rather steep, tightly curved piece of track. The engine was yet another immigrant from Lancashire, having arrived on the Cumberland coast the previous November from the Walkden Railways where it had been domiciled from new in October 1950.

'Repulse' charges past the washer at Ladysmith, 28 August 1973.

Again on 28 August 1973, 'Repulse' has its saddle tank topped-up outside the shed. 'Repulse' is still in existence, having been transported to the Lakeside & Haverthwaite Railway, near Ulverston, in September 1976 (see page 5).

Left: Andrew Barclay 0-4-0ST works No. 1974, NCB No. 8, runs along the south side of the harbour at Whitehaven, towards the foot of the Howgill Brake, on 14 May 1971. Construction work to form the harbour, from what had hitherto been an open creek, began in 1634. It grew to such an extent that by the middle years of the eighteenth century it had become the third largest port in England, after London and Bristol, with a significant amount of coal for export, mainly destined for Ireland and some for the Isle of Man, passing along the quays, a trade that continued into the 1970s. On the far side of the harbour a number of NCB wagons can be seen biding time until their contents can be dropped into the hold of a ship. No. 8 was originally purchased from Andrew Barclay's in June 1931 by the Cowpen Coal Co. Ltd at Blyth, Northumberland. It had 16in. x 24in. outside cylinders, 3ft 7in. diameter wheels, and an open-back cab. It was moved from Bates Colliery at Blyth to Whitehaven, initially to Ladysmith, in October 1970. When employed at the harbour, the locomotives were maintained at the former William Colliery shed, near Whitehaven Bransty Station. William Colliery had closed back in 1955.

Opposite: Earlier the same day, with the tower of St James' Church, consecrated in July 1753, standing proud above the rooftops of Whitehaven, No. 8 skirts round the harbour with coal raised at Haig Colliery. As evidenced here, due to the tight curves that had to be negotiated only short wheelbased locomotives could be used on the harbour lines. The building in the left foreground was the fish office, while the large silo on the far side of the harbour was used for the storage of imported phosphate by Albright & Wilson, pending its transfer by road to their factory by Ladysmith Washery. Both buildings have since been demolished.

No. 8 exchanges greetings with Peckett Class W7 0-4-0ST works No. 2028, 'Victoria', built in 1942, on 13 May 1971. This engine had 14in. x 22in. outside cylinders and 3ft 2in. diameter wheels with a wheelbase of 5ft 6in. It was originally delivered to the Royal Ordnance Factory at Sellafield, nine miles south of Whitehaven, as an oil-burner complete with spark arrester, one of seventeen W7s bought between April 1941 and May 1943 by the Ministry of Supply for use at ROF establishments. It was later transferred to the ROF at Pembrey, near Llanelli in South Wales, where it was named 'Victoria', and then to ROF Fazakerley in Lancashire, before being purchased by the Whitehaven Harbour Commissioners in March 1959. 'Victoria' was hired to the NCB from 1967, having spells working from Ladysmith as well as on the harbour. 'Victoria' was cut up during September 1971.

Four locals seem quite oblivious of any danger as they amble around the harbour, while a 1966-registered Humber Sceptre car slowly edges forward over the uneven surface, just as No. 8 shunts a set of wagons near the Howgill Brake during May 1971. It's a scene that nowadays would, without doubt, incur the wrath of any visiting Health & Safety Executive official! The last steam locomotive to operate at the harbour was the former Solway Colliery Hudswell Clarke 0-4-0ST works No. 1814, 'Solway No. 2', built in 1948, during the summer of 1974. Today, there is very little commercial activity through the docks, coal exports, of course, being a thing of the past, and it is now mainly pleasure craft that frequent the restored harbour. Rightfully, Whitehaven's rich heritage is commemorated at The Beacon, a fine award-winning museum opened in July 1996 near the foot of the old Howgill Brake. Also worthy of note is the Miners Memorial Statue, unveiled at the harbour in June 2005 and poignantly entitled 'The End of an Era'. According to the statue's inscription, it was erected *In Celebration of the Past, To Inform the Present and Encourage the Future.*

Left: The coalfields in the Red Rose county were far more extensive than in Cumberland. For example, in 1950 there were sixty-three collieries spread across south and east Lancashire, with 46,938 men employed in the industry. Total output that year amounted to 12,270,529 tons. Earlier, in March 1929, six of the mining companies domiciled in the Manchester area amalgamated to form Manchester Collieries Ltd and one of the first tasks for the new company was to connect the 1913-opened Astley Green Colliery at Tyldesley, formerly owned by the Pilkington Colliery Co. Ltd, to the extensive Bridgewater Collieries railway, one mile to the east at Boothsbank, near Worsley. In NCB days this network became known as the Walkden Railways. In 1960 Astley Green had 2,299 men on its books and produced 705,000 tons of coal for domestic, gas and industrial purposes. It was one of four pits keeping the railway busy. However, ten years later, only Astley Green remained, and this too was closed down on 3 April 1970, with just the washery continuing in use for a few more months. Here, on 20 August that year, as four youngsters enjoy fishing the Bridgewater Canal, Hudswell Clarke-built 'Austerity' 0-6-0ST works No. 1776, 'Harry', built in 1944, goes about its daily duties. 'Harry' spent twenty years at various opencast coal disposal points in Lancashire and Yorkshire, before a short stint at Gin Pit Colliery, Tyldesley, preceded its transfer to the Walkden Railways early in 1966.

Opposite: On the same day, a more mature fisherman by the Bridgewater Canal, which in past years carried prodigious amounts of coal from the local pits, is momentarily distracted from his rod as 'Harry' returns to the colliery yard with a string of wagons collected from the sidings by the former Liverpool & Manchester Railway. To secure a firm foundation for this one-and-a-half-mile line across an area of peatbog it was necessary to lay hundreds of tree trunks and branches, topped with colliery waste, a method similar to that pioneered by George Stephenson in the 1820s in constructing the historic L&MR over Chat Moss.

In a number of places the Walkden Railway ran very near to residential properties, even close to the town centre at Walkden itself, resulting in numerous complaints to the NCB regarding the amount of black smoke discharged into the atmosphere by the hard-working locomotives, particularly following the passing of the Clean Air Act in 1956. An attempt to solve the problem in 1959 by adapting eight engines to burn a mixture of coke and coal met with little success (see page 7), following which, in 1961, after successful trials elsewhere, the NCB embarked on a programme of fitting some of the Walkden stock with a Giesl ejector. A major consideration was that a Giesl normally emitted a much cleaner exhaust than an engine with a conventional chimney and blastpipe, and coupled with a reduction in fuel costs and a slightly improved performance (see page 3), made the modification an attractive proposition. The first Walkden engine to receive the equipment was Hudswell Clarke 'Austerity' works No. 1778, 'Charles', built in 1944, followed by a further eight 'Austerities', along with Kerr Stuart Victory class 0-6-0T works No. 3068, 'Francis', built in 1917, which was regrettably scrapped in October 1968. Unfortunately, black smoke continued to be a source of irritation and the complaints continued, the local authority even bringing a court case against the NCB in September 1963. Here, Giesl-fitted 'Austerity' Hunslet works No. 3696, 'Respite', which came new to Walkden in October 1950, shunts the east end of the yard at Astley Green Colliery on 7 October 1970. Prominent on the skyline, on the right, is the spire of Worsley Parish Church.

A close-up portrait of 'Respite' coupled to a seven-plank wooden wagon at Astley Green on 7 October 1970. Note the distinctive oblong Giesl ejector and the torpedo-like water tank, adapted from an old boiler, on the right.

Left: Again on 7 October 1970, 'Respite' is reflected in the waters of the Bridgewater Canal against a backdrop of the colliery buildings at Astley Green.

Opposite: On the very murky morning of Thursday 8 October 1970 at Astley Green, 'Respite' shunts a long link of NCB internal wagons. The washery had been closed down the previous Friday and locomotive work was destined to finish once clearing operations had been concluded. A few days later, the last two locomotives based at Astley Green, 'Harry' and 'Respite', made their melancholy way to Walkden for storage. The tall chimney, nearest the camera in the centre of the picture, was latterly the escape route for the fumes from a large boiler erected in 1960/61, housed in the building to the right of the chimney, that burned coal slurry and methane. Behind, partly hidden, the two older chimneys continued to provide the outlets for a bank of sixteen Lancashire boilers when needed, although six had been converted to act as steam accumulators to maintain the supply to the winding engines from the replacement boiler. After 1970 most of the buildings were erased, the main exception being No. 1 pit headgear (the one furthest from the camera) and its associated winding house, together with the original massive Yates and Thom of Blackburn twin-tandem compound 35in. diameter (high pressure), 60in. diameter (low pressure), 72in. stroke engine that once lowered the cages up to 2,619ft below the surface. These are now important features of the Astley Green Colliery Museum.

The ex-Manchester Collieries four-and-a-half-mile line from Astley Green Colliery to Linnyshaw Moss sidings, near Kearsley - from which point the wagons were taken forward by British Railways either to the Central Electricity Generating Board's Kearsley Power Station or to other recipients by way of a connection with the ex-Lancashire & Yorkshire Railway Manchester to Bolton line - was last used at the beginning of October 1970. Two months earlier, on Wednesday 19 August 1970, the Rochdale-based Roch Valley Railway Society organised a tour of the system behind 'Warrior', a Giesl ejector-fitted 'Austerity' which had been at Walkden since delivered new from the Hunslet factory in September 1954 as their works No. 3823. With fifty or so enthusiastic passengers standing in the Spartan surrounds of three NCB wooden wagons, the special is seen at Ashton's Field, between Little Hulton and Farnworth, the train then having to reverse in order to reach Linnyshaw Moss. The colliery at Ashton's Field had closed in 1929 although it was retained for pumping purposes until 1968, the site also being utilised for a blending plant from the mid-1930s.

The small cluster of former Manchester Collieries buildings at Walkden, seven miles or so north west of the centre of Manchester, was usually referred to as Walkden Yard. They were used by the NCB as a central workshop facility, and from 1947 over sixty steam locomotives visited the site for overhaul or repair (many on several occasions with a few receiving attention six or more times), two even coming from Mountain Ash in South Wales in 1971. A new repair shop was completed in 1953 and seen here, dismantled inside the building on 23 January 1975 after its escapade at Haig Colliery, Whitehaven, the previous November (see page 12), is Hunslet 'Austerity' works No. 3696, 'Respite', built in 1950. The renovated locomotive was despatched to Bickershaw Colliery, Leigh, later that year.

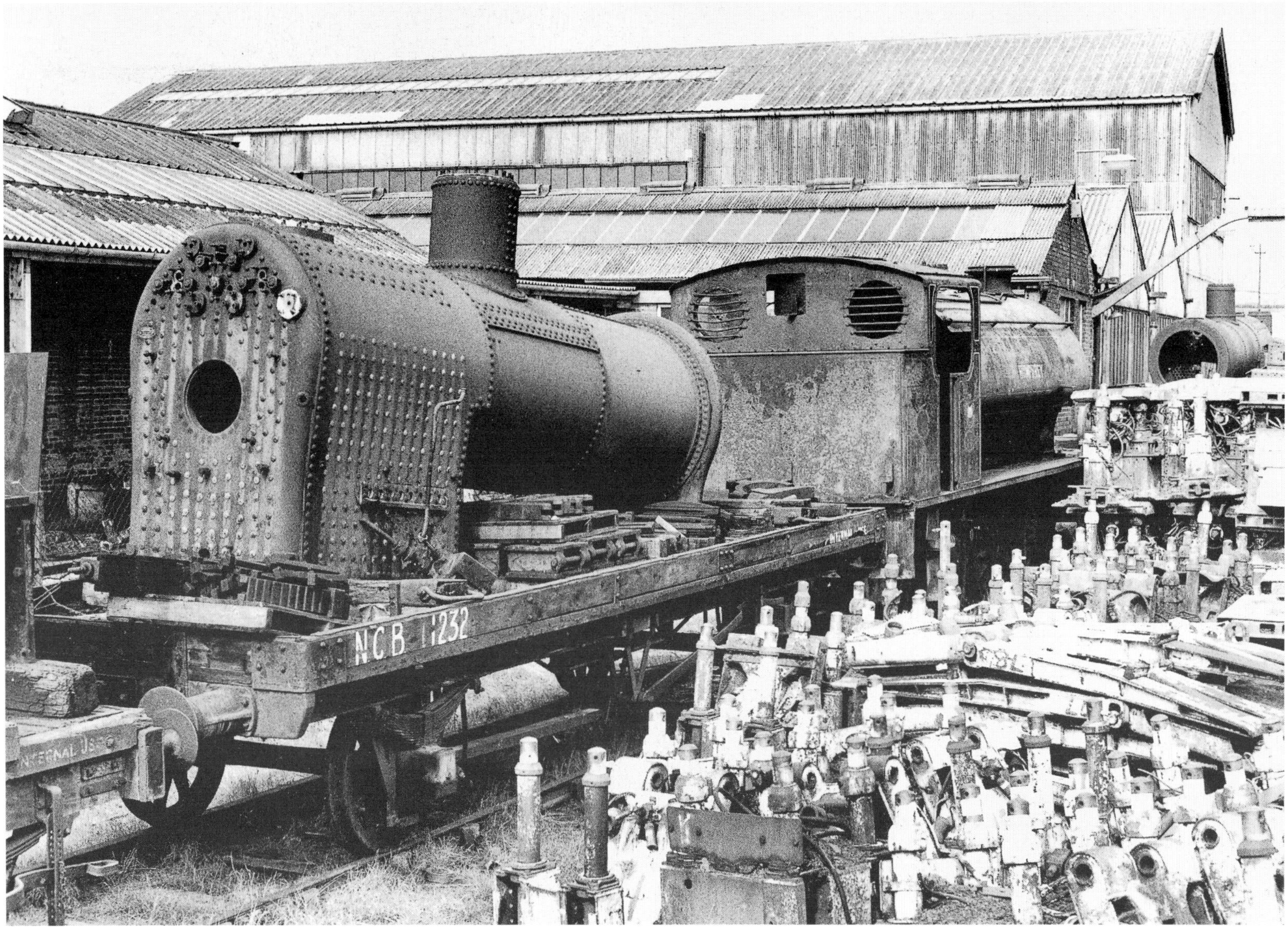
NCB 1232

Opposite: On the same day as the photograph on the previous page, biding time in the yard at Walkden is 'Humphrey', an 'Austerity' constructed by Robert Stephenson & Hawthorns of Newcastle-upon-Tyne in 1945, works No. 7293, together with a couple of boilers. Initially, 'Humphrey' was delivered to the Longmoor Military Railway in Hampshire as WD No. 71484, where it was stored prior to being sold to Manchester Collieries the following March. It was employed at a number of collieries in Lancashire before it arrived at Walkden from the Gin Railways shed at Tyldesley in December 1967. It was transported to J.K. Holt Gordon Ltd at Westhoughton, near Bolton, for scrapping in February 1976. Incidentally, on display by the entrance to what was Holt Gordon's yard, now J. Doyle Ltd, is Avonside Engine Company 0-6-0ST works No. 1600, built in 1912 and saved from the oxyacetylene torch after being bought from Cronton Colliery at Whiston, near St Helens, in June 1965.

Right: Photographed on 23 March 1974, 'Warrior' rests inside the two-road engine shed that was once the nerve centre of the Walkden Railways, while fellow 'Austerity' 'Harry' (see page 30) stands out of sight on the right. The latter eventually left for preservation in February 1976 and is currently under restoration at Bryn Engineering at Pemberton, near Wigan. After the railway closed in 1970, 'Warrior' was retained and steamed very occasionally in order to shunt the yard. In August 1977 it was transferred to Bickershaw Colliery at Leigh. Walkden Yard closed in 1986, with the area now largely covered by a housing development.

Bedford Colliery at Leigh, known locally as 'Woodend', was founded by John Speakman during the mid–1870s and continued in the ownership of the family, latterly as a private limited company, until it was absorbed by the newly incorporated Manchester Collieries in March 1929. In 1950 the NCB employed 906 men at Bedford, with over 221,000 tons of coal being hoisted to the surface for sale to domestic and industrial consumers. Ten years later, in 1960, the number of workers had been reduced to 662 although the colliery yielded a slightly higher output of 226,000 tons. Overlooked by the winding wheels, which were able to lower the cages some 2,600ft below the surface, Hunslet 'Austerity' works No. 3697 'Renown', built in 1950, has its bunker replenished from a wooden wagon on 2 August 1967. The following three photographs at Bedford were all taken on the same day.

Here, above the two surface workers on the right, the tender of BR Stanier Class 8F 2-8-0 No. 48749 can just be seen in the exchange sidings by the former London & North Western Railway Pennington to Tyldesley line, as 'Renown' reverses back towards the colliery. To the right of the 'Austerity', beyond the footbridge, is the weighbridge hut, the notice above the steps clearly stating that 'maximum speed of locomotives and wagons over this weighbridge must not exceed 2 miles per hour'. After it had given eighteen years efficient service to various collieries in the area, 'Renown' was dismantled at Walkden in October 1968. Likewise No. 48749 met its end the same year after a slightly longer active life that lasted just over 21 years, being scrapped by John Cashmore Ltd at Tipton, near Wolverhampton, during the summer of 1968.

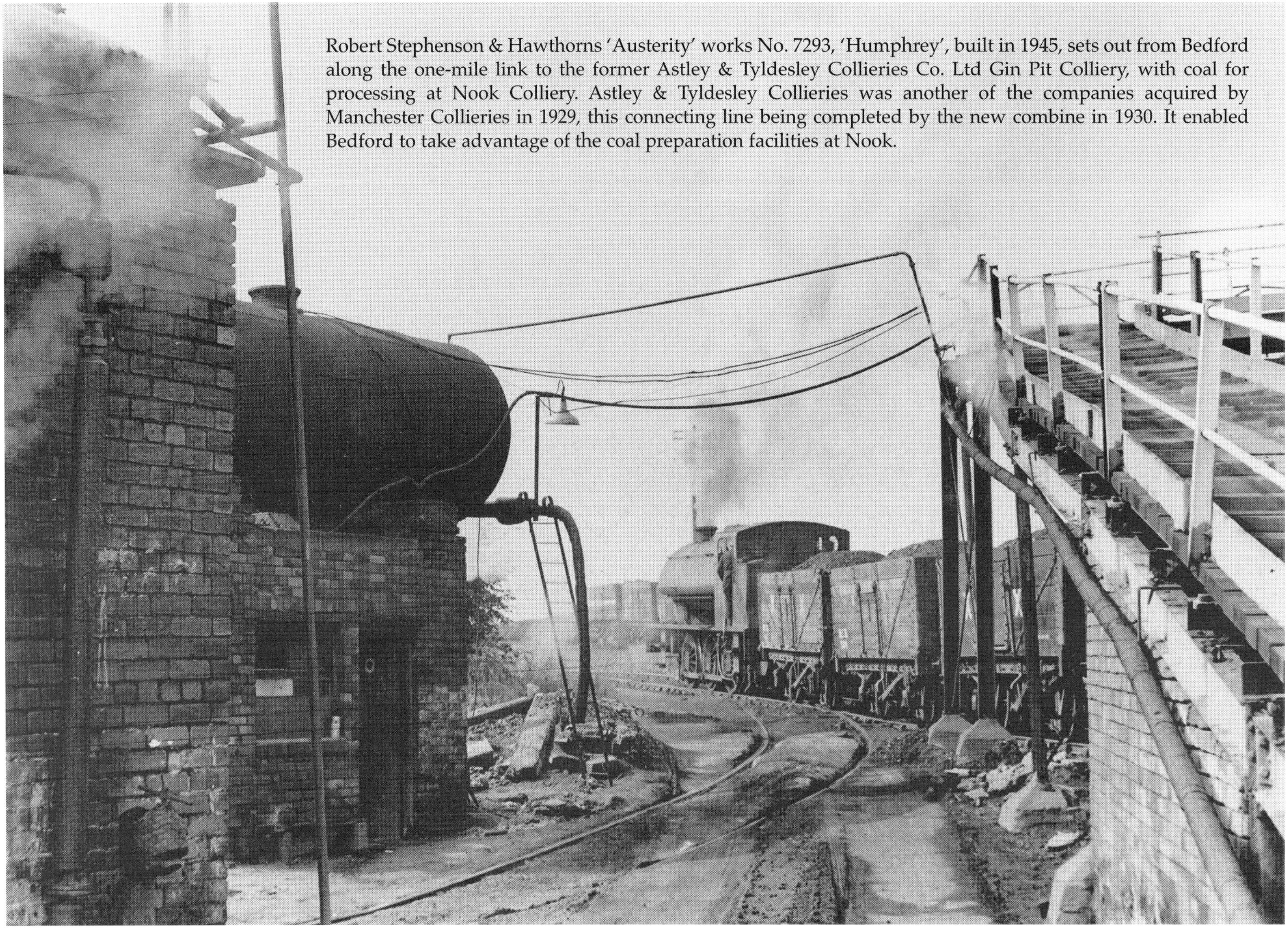

Robert Stephenson & Hawthorns 'Austerity' works No. 7293, 'Humphrey', built in 1945, sets out from Bedford along the one-mile link to the former Astley & Tyldesley Collieries Co. Ltd Gin Pit Colliery, with coal for processing at Nook Colliery. Astley & Tyldesley Collieries was another of the companies acquired by Manchester Collieries in 1929, this connecting line being completed by the new combine in 1930. It enabled Bedford to take advantage of the coal preparation facilities at Nook.

Later in the day, soon after leaving Bedford with a second load of coal for Nook, 'Humphrey' halts at a minor road crossing before being signalled across by the flagman. Bedford Colliery closed less than three months later on 28 October 1967, and with both Gin Pit and Nook already having stopped winding, the engine was moved to the Walkden Railways (see page 34/35).

Work on Bickershaw Colliery at Leigh, adjacent to a canal basin on the Leigh branch of the Leeds & Liverpool Canal, was started by Ackers Whitley & Co. Ltd in 1872, a company formed that year to carry forward the business of a long-established partnership of the same name. The canal basin was fed from a number of collieries situated alongside a two-mile mineral railway owned by Ackers Whitley, which at its northern end connected with the London & North Western Railway Wigan to Manchester line. During the early 1880s most of the Ackers Whitley line was taken over by the LNWR who were responsible for extending it south to Pennington, whereby trains could then continue to Kenyon Junction on the erstwhile Liverpool & Manchester Railway. Meanwhile, a connection had also been built from just north of the colliery to the 1879-opened Wigan Junction Railway (later the Great Central) Glazebrook to Wigan line.

In 1933 Ackers Whitley merged with its neighbour, the Abram Coal Co. Ltd, to form Bickershaw Collieries Ltd. Later, under the stewardship of the NCB in 1950, the pit found work for 2,734 men and raised 912,974 tons of coal for domestic and industrial use. During the 1950s a major reconstruction scheme was implemented with further work being carried out in the late 1960s, but even so by the 1970s the total number of employees had fallen to 1,370 with reduced production figures of approx 600,000 tons per annum. A further significant development in 1975 saw both Golborne Colliery, Golborne, and Parsonage Colliery, not far from the centre of Leigh, connected underground to Bickershaw, enabling the coal from all three collieries to be wound at the latter. By this time the only rail exit still in use was that to Wigan via the old LNWR line, the other routes from the colliery having been abandoned during the mid–1960s.

Photographed on 21 April 1976, Robert Stephenson & Hawthorns-built 'Austerity' works No. 7135, 'Gwyneth', built in 1944, makes a spirited departure from the colliery at the start of the steep one-mile climb up to Abram exchange sidings with a heavy load in tow. 'Gwyneth' has an interesting history, for as WD No. 75185 the engine was domiciled overseas in France for two years from May 1945. On its return it was purchased by the NCB and allocated first to Llay Main Colliery, north of Wrexham, and then to Gresford Colliery, Wrexham, before it eventually joined the stock at Bickershaw in January 1975. Not readily apparent today is the fact that, after 'Gwyneth' had been discarded by the NCB, many of its major components (boiler, cylinders etc) were used in 1985 in the creation of the replica Great Western Railway broad gauge width (7ft 0¼in) locomotive 'Iron Duke' for the National Railway Museum at York.

The Giesl-fitted 'Austerity', Hunslet works No. 3831, 'Spitfire', built for the NCB in September 1955, has a relatively easy task pushing three empty 16-ton capacity wagons to the back of the screens at Bickershaw on 18 August 1972. The wagons on the left were for NCB internal use only, readily identified as such by the large letter 'Xs' stencilled on the sides. During a lifespan of just over twenty years 'Spitfire' only ever worked in Leigh, spending about four years at Parsonage Colliery with the remainder at Bickershaw. It was scrapped on site by the contractors Mee & Cocker Ltd in March 1976.

Hunslet 'Austerity' works No. 3830, 'Hurricane', built in 1955, blasts its way up the final approach to the exchange sidings at Abram with coal from Bickershaw on 13 June 1974. Like its slightly younger sister, 'Spitfire', this engine was also employed throughout its life in Leigh, alternating between Parsonage and Bickershaw collieries. Jutting into the skyline in the background is the tall chimney and winding wheels at Golborne Colliery.

Right: Having deposited its wagons, 'Hurricane' runs light engine through the exchange sidings at Abram past BR Class 25 diesel-electric locomotive No. 25140, which had just arrived from Springs Branch shed, Wigan, again on the glorious summer evening of 13 June 1974. In August 1977 'Hurricane' was taken on a low loader to Walkden Central Workshops where it was cannibalised for spares. Its remains were finally disposed of in February 1981. In 1979 the nameplates from both 'Hurricane' and 'Spitfire' were presented to the Royal Air Force Museum at Cosford, near Wolverhampton.

Left: Driver Harold Gillibrand nonchalantly looks out from the cab of 'Rodney' in the exchange sidings at Abram, as the shunter and a couple of BR men attend to the brakes of a 'merry-go-round' wagon on 25 June 1973. 'Rodney', works No. 3695 built in 1950, was another of the batch of 'Austerities' purchased by the NCB in the 1950s from the Hunslet Engine Company. The engine spent most of its life in Leigh, having spells at Parsonage and Bedford collieries as well as at Bickershaw, relieved only by a couple of short stints on the Standish Railways, north of Wigan, during the 1950s. It was broken up at Bickershaw by Mee & Cocker during the spring of 1976.

Below: Hunslet works No. 3696, 'Respite', seen earlier on our travels at Astley Green Colliery, on the cliff tops at Whitehaven and in Walkden Central Workshops, takes water outside the two-road shed at Bickershaw on 29 June 1976. The driver keeps a watchful eye on proceedings from a lofty position halfway up the tower. The engine had joined the stock at Bickershaw only the previous year on completion of an overhaul at Walkden (see page 33). It is now at the Ribble Steam Railway in Preston.

Above: Nearing the end of another shift at Bickershaw, Harold Gillibrand cleans out the accumulated ash in the smokebox of 'Hurricane' before running it into the shed for the night on 2 June 1976.

The last steam locomotive to join the fleet of 'Austerities' at Bickershaw was the former Walkden Workshops shunter 'Warrior' (see page 35), Hunslet works No. 3823, built in 1954, which arrived in August 1977. Here, 'Warrior' moves a rake of empty 16-ton mineral wagons through the yard while behind some 'merry-go-round' wagons are being loaded from an overhead conveyor belt on 26 June 1978. The latter were destined for Fiddlers Ferry Power Station, between Warrington and Widnes. The building in the right foreground, near the shed, was used as a bothy by the enginemen. During the spring of 1979 steam's monopoly at Bickershaw came to an end with the debut of a pair of new diesels built by GEC Traction Ltd at Newton-le-Willows, although in the event steam was not totally dispensed with until the autumn of 1983. The colliery closed in March 1992. Recently some grandiose plans have been unveiled to reclaim the area and develop it for housing, retail and leisure purposes, while 'Warrior' can be seen at the headquarters of the Dean Forest Railway at Norchard, near Lydney, in Gloucestershire, where it arrived in September 1984.

Left: The sinking of Bold Colliery, St Helens, commenced in 1875, five years before it was acquired in 1880 by the owners of an adjacent pit, the Collins Green Colliery Co. Ltd, who operated the mine until 1940 when the liquidators were called in. In the event the pit was quickly reopened by another local company, the Sutton Heath & Lea Green Collieries Co. Ltd. A few years later, in 1947, its first year under state ownership, Bold produced 210,000 tons of coal for gas, household, manufacturing and steam purposes with 910 men listed on the payroll. During the early 1950s the NCB embarked on a major reconstruction scheme, including a new coal preparation plant and a more expansive network of sidings on the surface. By 1957 the number of employees had increased to over 1,800, the pit lifting 749,000 tons of coal that year, most of it being carried by a conveyor belt to the nearby 1953-opened Bold Power Station. A rail connection was provided for emergency use.

Concurrent with the modernisation of the colliery, Bold took delivery of its first diesel in 1957, steam then being relegated to a standby role. However, early in 1974, when the colliery was still loading over 700,000 tons of coal per annum onto the conveyors, BR decided to introduce 'merry-go-round' wagons on some of its Bold contracts and with the diesels being unable to handle these larger capacity wagons, steam made a welcome renaissance. Here, on 20 August 1974, the shunter attaches a couple of 'merry-go-round' wagons to Hunslet 'Austerity' works No. 3694, 'Whiston'. The engine, new to the NCB in October 1950, was always employed in the St Helens area, first for a short time on the Haydock Railways before moving to Cronton Colliery at Whiston. It was reallocated to Bold during the second half of 1961, receiving the name 'Whiston' in about 1965. Note the cast Hunslet plate on the side of the bunker stating the works number and year of manufacture and the NCB crest stencilled on the side of the cab.

Opposite: While preparations continued apace at Bold Colliery for the Rocket 150 celebrations the following weekend (see page 5), 'Joseph' was observed transferring some empty 16-ton mineral wagons from the exchange sidings to the colliery yard on 20 May 1980. Bold Power Station provides the backcloth, while the track on the near side of the fence once belonged to the Liverpool & Manchester Railway. This particular 'Austerity' was handed over by Hunslet as their works No. 3163 to the Ministry of Supply in April 1944. Following a number of Army postings as WD No. 75113, it was repurchased by Hunslet in October 1962, given a complete rebuild in their Leeds factory and allocated the new works No. 3885 in 1964. The engine was then loaned for one year from May 1965 to Coventry Homefire Plant, after which it languished in Leeds until July 1970 when it was bought by the NCB. Following an overhaul at Walkden Central Workshops it went to Gresford Colliery, Wrexham, in November 1970 where it was named 'Alison'. It arrived at Bold in 1974. In 1980 the engine had the distinction of being the last steam locomotive to receive attention at Walkden where it was renamed 'Joseph' on 15 February, just prior to returning to Bold.

Left: Coaling the easy way! After the midday lunch break on 20 August 1974, a mechanical shovel is used to feed the necessary fuel into the bunker of 'Whiston' at Bold Colliery, while the shunter assists the driver by taking the opportunity to oil round the motion.

Below: During the afternoon shift, 'Whiston' goes about the task of transferring 'merry-go-round' wagons, two at a time, up the short, sharp incline to the exchange sidings. Later in the day the wagons were collected by a BR Class 47 diesel locomotive and taken to one of the local power stations.